The Big Hungry Hairy Green Monster
Copyright © 2013 by Patty Smith
Illustrator: James Gage

ISBN-13   978-0615762685
ISBN-10   0615762689

Registered in Library of Congress
ISBN- 0615762689

For information contact
questionsandmore13@yahoo.com

BURP-BURP-BURP

The Big Hungry Hairy Green Monster

TOOT-TOOT-TOOT

Once upon a time, there was a big old house, on a big hill, with trees blowing in the breeze. And this big old house, had a big old basement, but me oh my, down in this big old basement was a mighty dusty-dungeon, with black, rusty-dusty bars.

And in the corner of the big old basement, in the mighty dusty-dungeon, lived The Big Hungry Hairy Green Monster, with big round purple eyes. But me oh my, The Big Hungry Hairy Green Monster, had his big round purple eyes closed tight. He was fast asleep, and he never-never got to eat.

Then one day from inside the mighty dusty-dungeon, The Big Hungry Hairy Green Monster's big round purple eyes suddenly opened, and his big tummy was very-very hungry, and his throat was very-very dry.

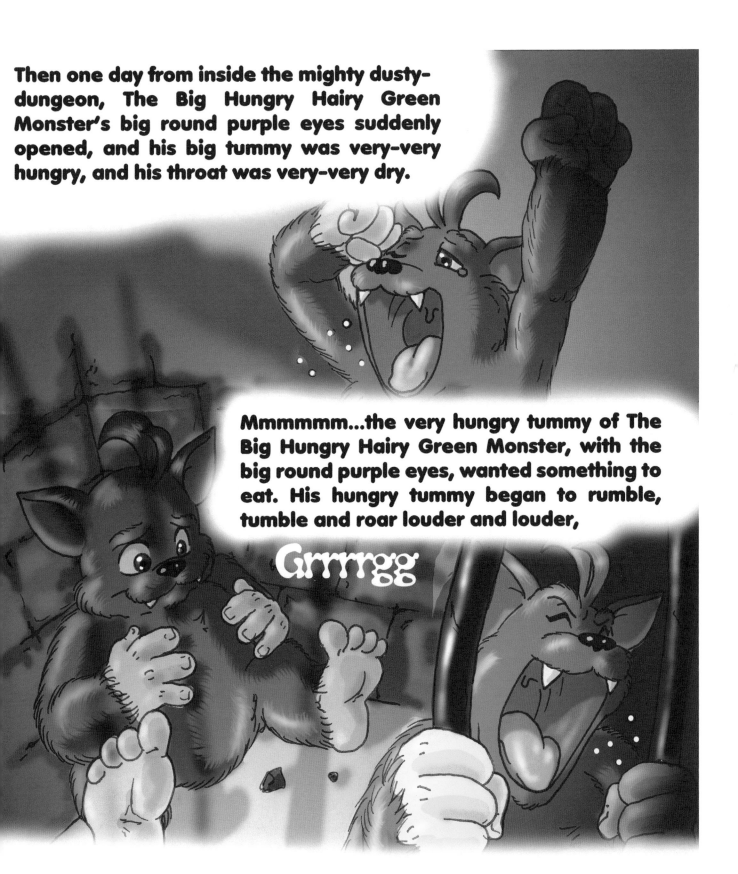

Mmmmmm...the very hungry tummy of The Big Hungry Hairy Green Monster, with the big round purple eyes, wanted something to eat. His hungry tummy began to rumble, tumble and roar louder and louder,

Grrrrgg

and The Big Hungry Hairy Green Monster, began to rattle and shake the black, rusty-dusty bars, crying out. "Let me out. Let me out, I am as hungry as can be, I need to feed me!"

Suddenly like magic in the night, the black, rusty-dusty bars opened. The Big Hungry Hairy Green Monster's big round purple eyes began to dance as he pranced his way out of the mighty dusty-dungeon. His big feet thumped loudly all the way up the winding steps.

When he found the cold-gold refrigerator, his big round purple eyes lit up bright in sheer delight, and he began to dance and prance around the room. Mummmmm...his shiny black nose smelled the food and his mouth began to water. He was very hungry and he did not wait. He ate and ate.

Mummmmm...he ate and he ate. He ate all the chocolate cake. Then gulp-gulp-gulp, he guzzled down a gallon of white milk, without so much as a fight.

But me oh my, out from nowhere, his big, full hungry tummy, began to rumble, tumble and roar, rumble, tumble and roar, and out from nowhere, he went burp-burp- burp and toot-toot-toot-burp-burp-burp and toot-toot-toot.

Mummmmm...only now, he was hungrier than ever. His big, hungry tummy began to rumble, tumble and roar louder than before. But-but...there were no more cookies! But...but there was no more cake! What! There was no more milk!

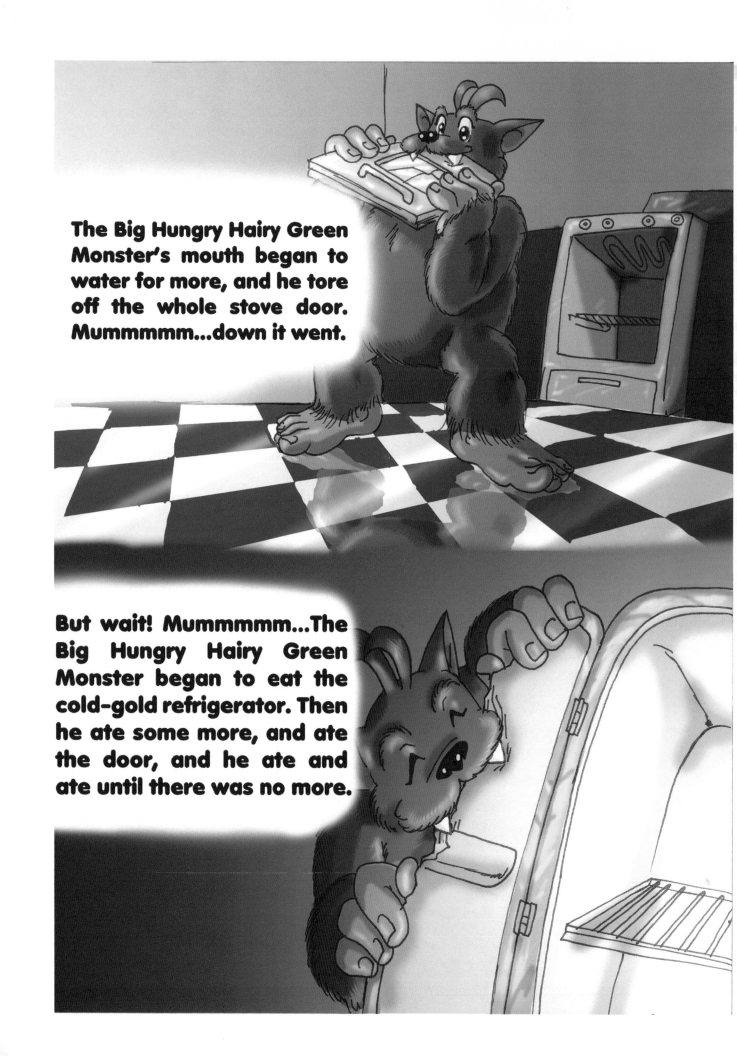

The Big Hungry Hairy Green Monster's mouth began to water for more, and he tore off the whole stove door. Mummmmm...down it went.

But wait! Mummmmm...The Big Hungry Hairy Green Monster began to eat the cold-gold refrigerator. Then he ate some more, and ate the door, and he ate and ate until there was no more.

His big, hungry tummy began to rumble, tumble and roar louder than before. And out from nowhere, he went burp-burp-burp and toot-toot-toot-burp-burp-burp and toot-toot-toot. But me oh my, his tummy was as big as a ball, and he couldn't stand tall. He began to roll all the way back down to the mighty dusty-dungeon, and like magic in the night, the black, rusty-dusty bars closed behind him.

Now, with all that The Big Hungry Hairy Green Monster had eaten, he slept and he slept. So as this story goes, no one heard from The Big Hungry Hairy Green Monster, for a long-long time, until, a hundred years later,

like magic in the night, he suddenly opened his big round purple eyes. Mummmmm...The Big Hungry Hairy Green Monster was ready to eat some more!

The BIG Hungry Hairy Green Monster

BURP-BURP-BURP

The Big Hungry Hairy Green Monster Ventures out

TOOT-TOOT-TOOT

On the big hill, with all the trees blowing in the breeze, it was inside the big old house, where The Big Hungry Hairy Green Monster slept, with his big round purple eyes closed tight. He was fast asleep down in the big old basement, in the mighty dusty-dungeon, with the black, rusty-dusty bars closed. Once again, his big round purple eyes suddenly opened. Mummmmm...his big, hungry tummy was very-very hungry, and his throat was very-very dry. His big, hungry tummy began to rumble, tumble and roar.

Mummmmm...he was so very hungry, he began to rattle and shake the black, rusty-dusty bars, yelling out. "Let me out, let me out; I am as hungry as can be, I need to feed me!" Like magic in the night, the black, rusty-dusty bars suddenly opened, and his big round purple eyes began to dance,

as he pranced his way out of the mighty dusty-dungeon. His big feet thumped loudly up the winding staircase, past where the cold-gold refrigerator and gold stove once stood, and he skipped his way right out the door.

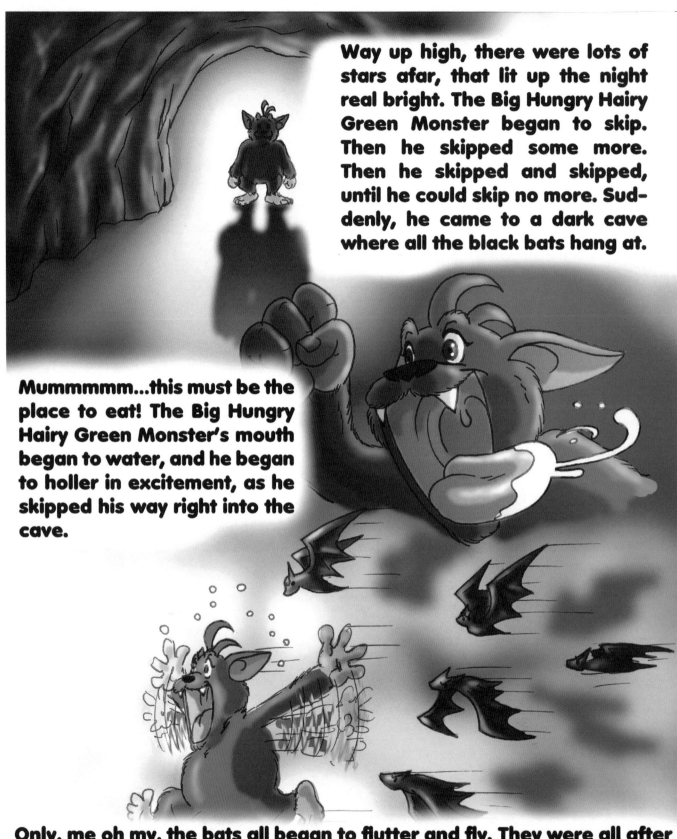

Way up high, there were lots of stars afar, that lit up the night real bright. The Big Hungry Hairy Green Monster began to skip. Then he skipped some more. Then he skipped and skipped, until he could skip no more. Suddenly, he came to a dark cave where all the black bats hang at.

Mummmmm...this must be the place to eat! The Big Hungry Hairy Green Monster's mouth began to water, and he began to holler in excitement, as he skipped his way right into the cave.

Only, me oh my, the bats all began to flutter and fly. They were all after The Big Hungry Hairy Green Monster! Ohhhhh The Big Hungry Hairy Green Monster was so afraid, that he ran as fast as he can. Even faster, than the gingerbread man, ducking all the way, never looking back to where the black bats were hanging at.

His big, hungry tummy began to rumble, tumble and roar, he was so very-very hungry. His big round purple eyes were searching and searching for food. His shiny black nose was sniffing, when suddenly he smelled some flowering buds. Mummmmm...only there were no buzzing bees, making any honey in the flowering trees.

Then across the way, he stood up taller and spotted the water and he began to holler in delight. Mummmmm...when his shiny black nose smelled the fish, his mouth began to water, and his big, hungry tummy began to rumble, tumble and roar some more.

Mummmmm...into the water he dove big tummy and all. He began jumping up and down, grabbing for the fish, only he missed. But-but...in all his excitement, suddenly, all the fish were gone and nowhere to be found. By now, The Big Hungry Hairy Green Monster was so hungry; his mouth began to water even more.

But-but there on the sand, here and there, he spotted some colorful beach balls, lying all around. Mummmmm...they looked as tasty as could be, and me oh my, he ate all three.

Oh, but his big tummy was so full of air; he began to float up higher and higher. He was so high up in the sky, The Big Hungry Hairy Green Monster didn't know why. So like the bats, he tried to flutter and fly.

Only, me oh my, he began to float up higher over the trees in the windy breeze. He didn't say wheeeee...instead, his big round purple eyes got bigger, and he was so afraid, he cried.

"Please...please help me." Suddenly, his big, round tummy began to rumble, tumble and roar, rumble, tumble and roar and out from nowhere in midair, he went, burp-burp-burp and toot-toot-toot-burp-burp-burp and toot-toot-toot.

His big tummy had let out all the air and he began to tumble down into the tall trees, blowing in the breeze, next to the big old house, on the big hill. "Ouch" he cried, "Ouch-ouch-ouch." But his big round purple eyes were no longer afraid,

as he huffed and puffed his way back to the mighty dusty-dungeon. Oh, but he was so very-very tired, that he closed his big round purple eyes and curled himself up, into one giant ball. And like magic in the night, the black, rusty-dusty bars closed behind him, and The Big Hungry Hairy Green Monster, slept another hundred years.

So as this story goes, no one heard from The Big Hungry Hairy Green Monster, for a long-long time. Until a hundred years later, like magic in the night, he suddenly opened his big round purple eyes.

Mummmmm...The Big Hungry Hairy Green Monster was ready to eat some more!

The BIG Hungry Hairy Green Monster

BURP-BURP-BURP

The Big Hungry Hairy Green Monster Loses his way home

TOOT-TOOT-TOOT

On the big hill, with all the trees blowing in the breeze, it was inside the big old house, where The Big Hungry Hairy Green Monster slept, with his big round purple eyes closed tight. He was fast asleep, down in the big old basement, in the mighty dusty-dungeon, with the black, rusty-dusty bars closed. Suddenly, his big round purple eyes opened. His tummy was very-very hungry, and his mouth was very-very dry and his hungry tummy began to rumble, tumble and roar.

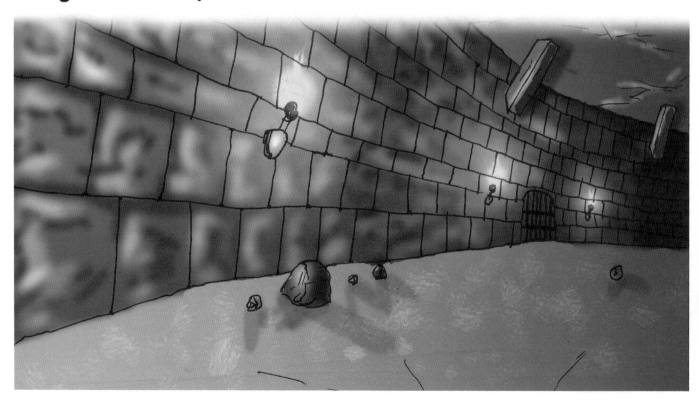

Once again, he began to rattle and shake the black, rusty-dusty bars, yelling out. "Let me out, let me out; I am as hungry as can be, I need to feed me!" Like magic in the night, the black, rusty-dusty bars suddenly opened. His big round purple eyes began to dance and he pranced his way out of the mighty dusty-dungeon. His big feet loudly thumped up the winding staircase, past where the cold-gold refrigerator and gold stove once stood. And just like before, he skipped his way right out the door!

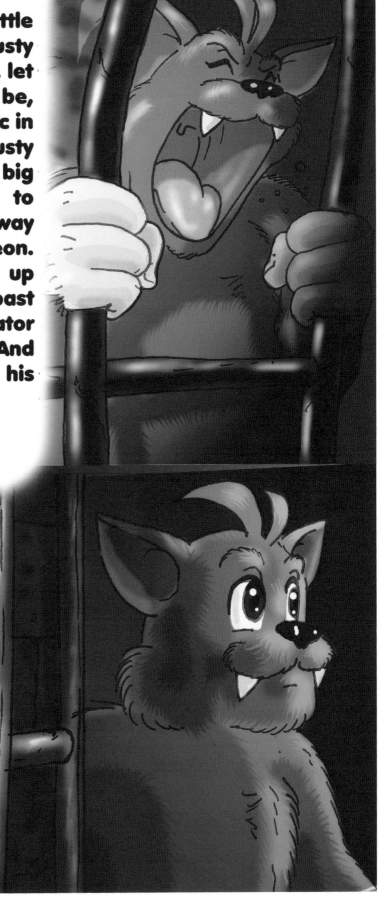

Before long, The Big Hungry Hairy Green Monster's shiny black nose smelled some food and his mouth began to water. Mummmmm...his big, hungry tummy began to rumble, tumble and roar. When he climbed into the back of a red wooden egg truck, all the feathery chickens began to cluck up a storm. Mummmmm...with the feathery chickens' heads sticking out from the wooden cages, pecking and clucking, The Big Hungry Hairy Green Monster ducked out of their way.

Then, he began to eye the cartons of eggs, stacked up high in rows of eight. Mummmmm...the tummy of The Big Hungry Hairy Green Monster, began to rumble, tumble and roar, rumble, tumble and roar.

Mummmmm...he was so very-very hungry, he gobbled the eggs and ate and ate. He ate all the eggs one by one, until they were gone. Now with all the cartons lying empty all around, he tried to put his feet back on the ground. Only his tummy was so big, he fell back down. Suddenly, his big tummy began to rumble, tumble and roar. It rumbled, tumbled and roared, and out from nowhere, he went burp-burp-burp and toot-toot-toot-burp-burp-burp and toot-toot-toot.

Suddenly, the red wooden truck began to move, bumpity bump, bumpity bump, and The Big Hungry Hairy Green Monster's big tummy was being tossed up and down round and round, and the eggs down inside his big tummy, all turned into one, big, pound of scrambled eggs.

Suddenly, the red wooden truck came to a stop, while his feathery friends were still clucking up a storm. Now the big tummy, of The Big Hungry Hairy Green Monster, was as big as a ball and he couldn't stand tall and he rolled his way out of the red wooden truck. Bye chickens he waved, bye bye, but suddenly, he was looking all around, and the big old house on the big hill, where all the trees blew in the breeze, was no where to be found. Oh me oh my, now he was lost, no matter how many times he spun around and around.

He was so afraid, he let out a sigh and his big round purple eyes began to cry. But then, he saw a big white castle that sparkled in the night. It too, had a mighty dusty-dungeon, and the black, rusty-dusty bars, were wide open for The Big Hungry Hairy Green Monster to call his new home. Only-only wait, something dark and scary, was in the corner of the mighty dusty-dungeon. Suddenly, it was coming towards him, closer and closer. The Big Hungry Hairy Green Monster's big round purple eyes got bigger. He was so afraid, he cried. "Please...please help me," and he began to shake and shake.

But-but then wait! It was a Beautiful Pink Furry Monster, with big round purple eyes and long black eyelashes. The Big Hungry Hairy Green Monster squeaked, aweeeee-eeeee!

Aweeeee-eeeee and the Beautiful Pink Furry Monster's long black eyelashes began to flutter and she went eeeeee, just as he. But me oh my, now The Big Hungry Hairy Green Monster was not hungry...he was in loveeeee. Eeeeee-aweeeee he was standing tall, until he began to stumble and fall over his own big feet. Then, the Beautiful Pink Furry Monster, put her hand up to her mouth and began to wiggle and giggle. Her long black eyelashes began to flutter, and they both wanted to be together forever.

Eeeeee-aweeeee, The Big Hungry Hairy Green Monster ran out of the dungeon. He was so happy he skipped and skipped. Then he skipped some more, until he could skip no more. He passed an apple orchard where the apples hung green. So instead of eating the apples, he got down on his knees and pulled out a patch of weeds and clover, nearly knocking him over.

Skipping back to the Beautiful Pink Furry Monster, there, on the castle's windowsill, me oh my...sat a yummy blueberry pie! Mummmmm...
    When The Big Hungry Hairy Green Monster shared the weeds and yummy pie with the Beautiful Pink Furry Monster, her big round purple eyes began to dance, and her black eyelashes began to flutter and together they ate and ate.

Mummmmm...both of their tummies were as big as a ball and they couldn't stand tall. Suddenly out from nowhere, the big tummy of The Big Hungry Hairy Green Monster began to rumble, tumble and roar and he went burp-burp-burp and toot-toot-toot. Then, the tummy of the Beautiful Pink Furry Monster, began to jingle, jangle and roar and out from nowhere, she went, tootally-toot-tootally-toot and burpsy-burpsy. But me oh my, they were as happy as could be.

But later, inside the big white castle that sparkled in the night, down in the mighty dusty-dungeon, The Big Hungry Hairy Green Monster, and the Beautiful Pink Furry Monster were fast asleep. But in the arms of the Beautiful Pink Furry Monster...

laid one, two, three, three cute babies, all as fuzzy as can be. One was pink like mommy and one was green like dad and even though one had pink and green polka dots, it didn't make them sad. And like magic in the night, the black, rusty-dusty bars never closed behind them.

46957

Suid

18406744R00018

Made in the USA
Charleston, SC
01 April 2013